MW01104414

Fun with Light

Written by Maria Gordon
and
Illustrated by Mike Gordon

Thomson Learning
New York

Simple Science

Float and Sink
Fun with Light

First published in the
United States in 1995 by
Thomson Learning
115 Fifth Avenue
New York, NY 10003

First published in Great Britain in 1994 by Wayland (Publishers) Limited

Library of Congress Cataloging-in-Publication Data

Gordon, Maria.
  Fun with light / written by Maria Gordon and
illustrated by Mike Gordon.
          p.   cm. — (Simple science)
  Includes index.
  ISBN 1-56847-284-6. — ISBN 1-56847-308-7 (pbk.)
  1. Light—Juvenile literature. 2. Light—Experiments—Juvenile
literature. [1. Light. 2. Light—Experiments. 3. Experiments.]
I. Gordon, Mike, ill. II. Title. III. Series: Simple science
(New York, N.Y.)
QC360.G67   1995
535—dc20   94-25645

Printed in Italy

Contents

Light is a kind of energy.
We call it energy because it
makes things happen.

Light helps us see.
It helps plants grow.
Sunlight can burn
things – even our skin.

4

Most light comes from the sun. Sunlight does not reach us at night, so it is dark. At night, we have to use light from other things.

Lightning, stars, and fire
all give off light.

Humans put light where they need it: in houses, along streets, and on cars.

7

Long ago, cave people made light with fire.
Some burned animal fat in bowls.

Later, people used candles and lamps. These worked by burning wax, oil, or gas.

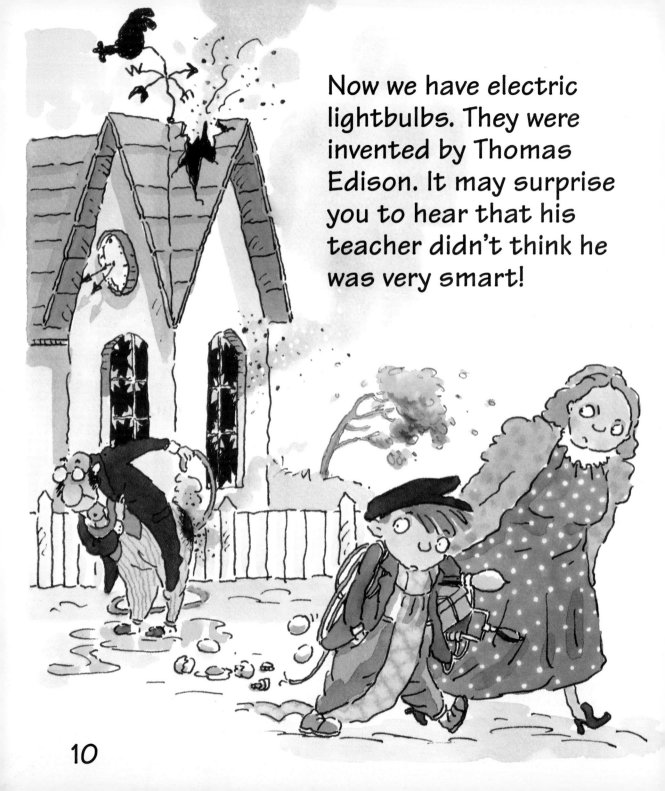

Now we have electric lightbulbs. They were invented by Thomas Edison. It may surprise you to hear that his teacher didn't think he was very smart!

Many bulbs have a long, curly wire inside them that gets very hot and gives off light. Some bulbs have paint or gas that glows inside them.

Light is moving all the time. It travels very fast. In fact, if it were possible for you to travel at the speed of light, you could go around Earth eight times in a second.

Light travels in straight lines. In a dark room, shine a flashlight down a straight straw. What happens?

Now bend the straw. What happens?

Although light travels in straight lines, when it hits things, it bounces off them. This is called reflection.

Find a mirror, some shiny stones, white and colored paper, and some bicycle reflectors. Make a room dark. Shine a flashlight on the things you have found. Which ones reflect the most light?

Look in a mirror. Light bounces off you and onto the mirror.
The mirror bounces back the light so well that you can see yourself in it.

What other things make reflections you can see? What happens if the reflectors are curved or if they are smooth?

The moon does not
make light. It shines
because it reflects
the sun's light.

At night we
cannot see the
sun, but it is still
shining. Sunlight is
falling on the other side
of the world and on the moon.
They both reflect the sun's light.

When things do not reflect
light they soak it up.
Black things look black
because they soak up all
the light that hits them.

White things look
white because they
reflect most of the
light that hits them.

White light is made up of
all the other colors!

Rainbows happen when something makes the colors in white light spread out.

Raindrops can make light spread out. Can you think of other things that do this? (These pictures will help you.)

Try jumbling colors
to make white light.
Make a disk
like this.

Push a pencil
through the middle.

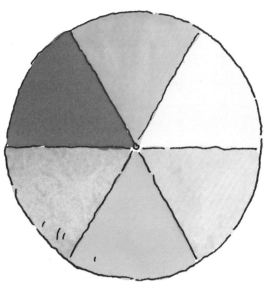

Watch what happens
when you spin the disk.

There are lots of things that you can see through. We say these things are transparent. Light goes through them.

Some things, like water and curved glass, let light through but make it bend.

Stand a straw in a glass of water. The bending light makes the straw look bent.

25

Can light go through YOU? Face a light (but do not look straight at it). Now look at the ground behind you. Is some of it darker than the ground in front? What shape is on the darker ground?

The dark shapes are
called shadows.

Make shadows with
different objects
and lights.

27

Plants soak up light and use it to make food. Without light, plants die.

Look at these pictures.
How many different ways
can you see light being used?

29

Additional Projects

Here are a few more projects to test out light. The projects go with the pages listed next to them. These projects are harder than the ones in the book, so be sure to ask a grown-up to help you.

4/5   Sunlight contains vitamins, so getting a little bit of sun every day is healthy. On the other hand, too much sun can damage your skin. Find out for your area how much sun is healthy and how much is harmful.

12/13   The sun gives light and heat to Earth and other planets. Look at a chart of the planets. Figure out which one gets the most light and heat from the sun, and which one gets the least light and heat from the sun. Is Earth the hottest planet?

16/17   Put a mirror in the middle of a wall and a chair anywhere else in the room. Turn off the lights. Try to light up the chair by shining a flashlight at the mirror. Draw a picture showing where you, the mirror, and the chair are when the light hits the chair.

18/19 The moon reflects the light of the sun. The moon appears in different shapes when sunlight is blocked from the moon by Earth. Draw moon shapes and think about where the sun and earth are to make the moon look like that.

20/21 Lay out different colored socks in the sun for an hour. Feel the socks. Which ones are warm? Which are cool?

26/27 Hang a large sheet of paper on a wall. Have a friend sit on a chair sideways to the wall. Shine a light on your friend's face. Move the light closer and farther away from the wall, and have your friend move closer and farther away. Watch the shadow change size. When you get it to the size you want, draw around the shadow of your friend's face.

28/29 Try growing bean sprouts on two saucers. Put a damp cloth on each saucer and sprinkle them with sprouts. Put one saucer in a bright, sunny spot and another in a dark closet. Keep the cloths damp. Which sprouts grow faster?

Other books to read

Davies, Kay and Oldfield, Wendy. **Light.** Starting Science. Milwaukee: Raintree Steck-Vaughn, 1991.

Livingston, Myra Cohn. **Light and Shadow.** New York: Holiday House, 1992.

Ward, Alan. **Light and Color.** Project Science. New York: Franklin Watts, 1992.

Jennings, Terry. **Light and Dark.** Junior Science. New York: Gloucester Press, 1991.

Index